Trots

A spectre would seem to be haunting the B...... ...... have the cheek to object to being paid nothing to work for Tescos – they are all "Trots". Teachers and parents object to school privatisation. They are all "Trots" too. And as for NHS privatisation – the "Trots" would seem to include all the professional bodies representing health professionals, patients groups and the trade unions inside and outside the Health Service.

Whoever these "Trots" are they do seem remarkably powerful. How come nobody has ever heard of them?

If you want to know what "Trots" believe then this little book will tell you. It is based on an historical public domain document drafted by Trotsky in 1938 yet when you read through it there are surprising echoes of the present day.

"Mankind's productive forces stagnate. Already new inventions and improvements fail to raise the level of material wealth. Conjunctural crises under the conditions of the social crisis of the whole capitalist system inflict ever-heavier deprivations and sufferings upon the general population. Growing unemployment, in its turn, deepens the financial crisis of the state and undermines the unstable monetary systems. Democratic regimes, as well as fascist, stagger on from one bankruptcy to another."

If we take it as read there are no Fascist regimes nowadays – just UKIP – the rest of this is very familiar. The people of Greece are expected to put up with cuts in wages and pensions while the bankers live the life of Riley. Millions of the 99 percent feel indignation about this.

And the transitional program has practical advice on how to turn this indignation into action and make the bosses pay for their crisis.

Derek McMillan

The Transitional Program

This work is public domain.

In exile from Stalin's Russia, Trotsky sought to create a worldwide socialist organisation. This founding statement explains why and explains the concept of a transitional program to take the movement forward.

Trotsky's supporters were hounded and murdered by Stalin's agents. Yet thousands of communists left Stalinist parties to rally behind Trotsky and his ideas. Read on to find out exactly what was so worrying for the Stalinists in Trotsky's ideas and what other socialists have found valuable about them.

Written by Leon Trotsky in 1938. Originally published in the May-June 1938 edition of *Bulletin of the Opposition* as a discussion document for the Founding Congress of the Fourth International (World Party of Socialist Revolution).

I have changed the spelling to UK English to make it easier for English readers, especially teachers, to understand. As a result of the 1950s, the upswing in capitalism on a world scale and the expansion of Stalinism into Eastern Europe, various organisations claim to continue the tradition on the Fourth International.

A good test would be to compare their program with the transitional program. Do they slavishly copy each detail whether appropriate or not; have they abandoned it altogether; or do they follow the method and the spirit of the Transitional Program adapted properly to the current century?The CWI can be contacted at the website http://www.worldsocialist-cwi.org/

[The Objective Prerequisites for a Socialist Revolution](#)

[The Proletariat and its Leadership](#)

[The Minimum Program and the Transitional Program](#)

[Sliding Scale of Wages and Sliding Scale of Hours](#)

[Trade Unions in the Transitional Epoch](#)

[Factory Committees](#)

["Business Secrets" and Workers' Control of Industry](#)

[Expropriation of Separate Groups of Capitalists](#)

[Expropriation of the Private Banks and State-ization of the Credit System](#)

[The Picket Line - Defence Guards/Workers' Militia—The Arming of the Proletariat](#)

[The Alliance of Workers and Farmers](#)

[The Struggle Against Imperialism and War](#)

[Workers' and Farmers' Government](#)

[Soviets](#)

[Backward Countries and the Program of Transitional Demand](#)

[The Program of Transitional Demands in Fascist Countries](#)

[The USSR and Problems of the Transitional Epoch](#)

[Against Opportunism and Unprincipled Revisionism](#)

[Against Sectarianism](#)

[Open the Road to the Woman Worker! Open the Road to the Youth!](#)

[Under the Banner of the Fourth International!](#)

The Objective Prerequisites for a Socialist Revolution

The world political situation as a whole is chiefly characterised by a historical crisis of the leadership of the proletariat.

The economic prerequisite for the proletarian revolution has already in general achieved the highest point of fruition that can be reached under capitalism. Mankind's productive forces stagnate. Already new inventions and improvements fail to raise the level of material wealth. Conjunctural crises under the conditions of the social crisis of the whole capitalist system inflict ever-heavier deprivations and sufferings upon the general population. Growing unemployment, in its turn, deepens the financial crisis of the state and undermines the unstable monetary systems. Democratic regimes, as well as fascist, stagger on from one bankruptcy to another.

The bourgeoisie itself sees no way out. In countries where it has already been forced to stake its last upon the card of fascism, it now toboggans with closed eyes toward an economic and military catastrophe. In the historically privileged countries, i.e., in those where the bourgeoisie can still for a certain period permit itself the luxury of democracy at the expense of national accumulations (Great Britain, France, United States, etc.), all of capital's traditional parties are in a state of perplexity bordering on a paralysis of will.

The "New Deal," despite its first period of pretentious resoluteness, represents but a special form of political perplexity, possible only in a country where the bourgeoisie succeeded in accumulating incalculable wealth. The present crisis, far from having run its full course, has already succeeded in showing that "New Deal" politics, like Popular Front politics in France, opens no new exit from the economic blind alley.

International relations present no better picture. Under the increasing tension of capitalist disintegration, imperialist antagonisms reach an impasse at the height of which separate clashes and bloody local disturbances (Ethiopia, Spain, the Far East, and Central Europe) must inevitably coalesce into a conflagration of world dimensions. The bourgeoisie, of course, is aware of the mortal danger to its domination represented by a new war. But that class is now immeasurably less capable of averting war than on the eve of 1914.

All talk to the effect that historical conditions have not yet "ripened" for socialism is the product of ignorance or conscious deception. The objective prerequisites for the proletarian revolution have not only "ripened"; they have begun to get somewhat rotten. Without a socialist revolution, in the next historical period at that, a catastrophe threatens the whole culture of mankind. The turn is now to the proletariat, i.e., chiefly to its revolutionary vanguard. The historical crisis of mankind is reduced to the crisis of the revolutionary leadership.

The Proletariat and its Leadership

The economy, the state, the politics of the bourgeoisie and its international relations are completely blighted by a social crisis, characteristic of a pre-Revolutionary state of society. The chief obstacle in the path of transforming the pre-Revolutionary into a revolutionary state is the opportunist character of proletarian leadership: its petty bourgeois cowardice before the big bourgeoisie and its perfidious connection with it even in its death agony.

In all countries the proletariat is racked by a deep disquiet. The multi-millioned masses again and again enter the road of revolution. But each time their own conservative bureaucratic machines block them.

The Spanish proletariat has made a series of heroic attempts since April 1931 to take power in its hands and guide the fate of society. However, its own parties (Social Democrats, Stalinists, Anarchists, and POUMists) — each in its own way acted as a brake and thus prepared Franco's triumphs.

In France, the great wave of "sit down" strikes, particularly during June 1936, revealed the wholehearted readiness of the proletariat to overthrow the capitalist system. However, the leading organisations (Socialists, Stalinists, Syndicalists) under the label of the Popular Front succeeded in canalising and damming, at least temporarily, the revolutionary stream.

The unprecedented wave of sit down strikes and the amazingly rapid growth of industrial unionism in the United States (the CIO) is the most indisputable expression of the instinctive striving of the American workers to raise themselves to the level of the tasks imposed on them by history. But here, too, the leading political organisations, including the newly created CIO, do everything possible to keep in check and paralyse the revolutionary pressure of the masses.

The definite passing over of the Comintern to the side of bourgeois order, its cynically counterrevolutionary role throughout the world, particularly in Spain, France, the United States and other "democratic" countries, created exceptional supplementary difficulties for the world proletariat. Under the banner of the October Revolution, the conciliatory politics practised by the "People's Front" doom the working class to impotence and clear the road for fascism.

"People's Fronts" on the one hand - fascism on the other: these are the last political resources of imperialism in the struggle against the proletarian revolution. From the historical point of view, however, both these resources are stopgaps. The decay of capitalism continues under the sign of the Phrygian cap in France as under the sign of the swastika in Germany. Nothing short of the overthrow of the bourgeoisie can open a road out.

The orientation of the general population is determined first by the objective conditions of decaying capitalism, and second, by the treacherous politics of the old workers' organisations. Of these factors, the first, of course, is the decisive one: the laws of history are stronger than the bureaucratic apparatus. No matter how the methods of the social betrayers differ — from the "social" legislation of Blum to the judicial frame-ups of Stalin - they will never succeed in breaking the revolutionary will of the proletariat. As time goes on, their desperate efforts to hold back the wheel of history will demonstrate more clearly to the general population that the crisis of the proletarian leadership, having become the crisis in mankind's culture, can be resolved only by the Fourth International.

The term "proletariat" for "working class" was common at the time of publication. The Labour Party has changed considerably becoming a purely capitalist party under Blair and experiencing a revival under Corbyn. - DM

The Minimum Program and the Transitional Program

The strategic task of the next period- pre-revolutionary period of agitation, propaganda and organisation - consists in overcoming the contradiction between the maturity of the objective revolutionary conditions and the immaturity of the proletariat and its vanguard (the confusion and disappointment of the older generation, the inexperience of the younger generation . It is necessary to help the general population in the process of the daily struggle to find the bridge between present demand and the socialist program of the revolution. This bridge should include a system of *transitional demands*, stemming from today's conditions and from today's consciousness of wide layers of the working class and unalterably leading to one final conclusion: the conquest of power by the proletariat.

Classical Social Democracy, functioning in an epoch of progressive capitalism, divided its program into two parts independent of each other: the *minimum program* which limited itself to reforms within the framework of bourgeois society, and the *maximum program* which promised substitution of socialism for capitalism in the indefinite future. Between the minimum and the maximum program no bridge existed. And indeed Social Democracy has no need of such a bridge, since the word *socialism* is used only for holiday speechifying. The Comintern has set out to follow the path of Social Democracy in an epoch of decaying capitalism: when, in general, there can be no discussion of systematic social reforms and the raising of he masses' living standards; when every serious demand of the proletariat and even every serious demand of the petty bourgeoisie inevitably reaches beyond the limits of capitalist property relations and of the bourgeois state.

The strategic task of the Fourth International lies not in reforming capitalism but in its overthrow. Its political aim is the conquest of power by the proletariat for the purpose of expropriating the bourgeoisie. However, the achievement of this strategic task is unthinkable without the most considered attention to all, even small and partial, questions of tactics. All sections of the proletariat, all its layers, occupations and groups should be drawn into the revolutionary movement. The present epoch is distinguished not for the fact that it frees the revolutionary party from day-to-day work but because it permits this work to be carried on indissolubly with the actual tasks of the revolution.

The Fourth International does not discard the program of the old "minimal" demands to the degree to which these have preserved at least part of their vital forcefulness. Indefatigably, it defends the democratic rights and social conquests of the workers. But it carries on this day-to-day work within the framework of the correct actual, that is, revolutionary perspective. Insofar as the old, partial, "minimal" demands of the masses clash with the destructive and degrading tendencies of decadent capitalism — and this occurs at each step - the Fourth International advances a system of *transitional demands,* the essence of which is contained in the fact that ever more openly and decisively they will be directed against the very bases of the bourgeois regime. The old "minimal program" is superseded by the *transitional program,* the task of which lies in systematic mobilisation of the masses for the proletarian revolution.

The transitional program does not mean that any demand which cannot be realised under capitalism is "transitional". Most politicians have pipe-dreams which cannot be realised under capitalism. A transitional demand is one which unites the working class and gives them a glimpse of what a new society would be like. - DM

Sliding Scale of Wages and Sliding Scale of Hours

Under the conditions of disintegrating capitalism, the general population continue to live the meagerised life of the oppressed, threatened now more than at any other time with the danger of being cast into the pit of pauperism. They must defend their mouthful of bread, if they cannot increase or better it. There is neither the need nor the opportunity to enumerate here those separate, partial demands which time and again arise on the basis of concrete circumstances - national, local, trade union. But two basic economic afflictions, in which is summarised the increasing absurdity of the capitalist system, that is, *unemployment* and *high prices,* demand generalised slogans and methods of struggle.

The Fourth International declares uncompromising war on the politics of the capitalists which, to a considerable degree, like the politics of their agents, the reformists, aims to place the whole burden of militarism, the crisis, the disorganisation of the monetary system and all other scourges stemming from capitalism's death agony upon the backs of the toilers. The Fourth International demands *employment* and *decent living conditions* for all.

Neither monetary inflation nor stabilisation can serve as slogans for the proletariat because these are but two ends of the same stick. Against a bounding rise in prices, which with the approach of war will assume an ever more unbridled character, one can fight only under the slogan of a *sliding scale of wages.* This means that collective agreements should assure an automatic rise in wages in relation to the increase in price of consumer goods.

Under the menace of its own disintegration, the proletariat cannot permit the transformation of an increasing section of the workers into chronically unemployed paupers, living off the slops of a crumbling society. The *right to employment is* the only serious right left to the worker in a society based upon exploitation. This right today is left to the worker in a society based upon exploitation. This right today is being shorn from him at every step. Against unemployment, "structural" as well as "conjunctural," the time is ripe to advance along with the slogan of public works, the slogan of a *sliding scale of working hours*. Trade unions and other mass organisations should bind the workers and the unemployed together in the solidarity of mutual responsibility. On this basis all the work on hand would then be divided among all existing workers in accordance with how the extent of the working week is defined. The average wage of every worker remains the same as it was under the old working week. Wages, under a strictly guaranteed *minimum,* would follow the movement of prices. It is impossible to accept any other program for the present catastrophic period.

Property owners and their lawyers will prove the "unrealisability" of these demands. Smaller, especially ruined capitalists, in addition will refer to their account ledgers. The workers categorically denounce such conclusions and references. The question is not one of a "normal" collision between opposing material interests. The question is one of guarding the proletariat from decay, demoralisation and ruin. The question is one of life or death of the only creative and progressive class, and by that token of the future of mankind. If capitalism is incapable of satisfying the demands inevitably arising from the calamities generated by it, then let it perish. "Realisability" or "unrealisability" is in the given instance a question of the relationship of forces, which can be decided only by the struggle. By means of this struggle, no matter what immediate practical successes may be, the workers will best come to understand the necessity of liquidating capitalist slavery.

Trade Unions in the Transitional Epoch

In the struggle for partial and transitional demands, the workers now more than ever before need mass organisations, principally trade unions. The powerful growth of trade unionism in France and the United States is the best refutation of the preachments of those ultra-left doctrinaires who have been teaching that trade unions have "outlived their usefulness."

The Bolshevik-Leninist stands in the front-line trenches of all kinds of struggles, even when they involve only the most modest material interests or democratic rights of the working class. He takes active part in mass trade unions for the purpose of strengthening them and raising their spirit of militancy. He fights uncompromisingly against any attempt to subordinate the unions to the bourgeois state and bind the proletariat to "compulsory arbitration" and every other form of police guardianship - not only fascist but also "democratic." Only on the basis of such work within the trade unions is successful struggle possible against the reformists, including those of the Stalinist bureaucracy. Sectarian attempts to build or preserve small "revolutionary" unions, as a second edition of the party, signify in actuality the renouncing of the struggle for leadership of the working class. It is necessary to establish this firm rule: self isolation of the capitulationist variety from mass trade unions, which is tantamount to a betrayal of the revolution, is incompatible with membership in the Fourth International.

At the same time, the Fourth International resolutely rejects and condemns trade union fetishism, equally characteristic of trade unionists and Syndicalists.

(a) Trade unions do not offer, and in line with their task, composition. and manner of recruiting membership, cannot offer a finished revolutionary program; in consequence, they cannot replace the *party*. The building of national revolutionary parties as sections of the Fourth International is the central task of the transitional epoch.

(b) Trade unions, even the most powerful, embrace no more than 20 to 25 percent of the working class, and at that, predominantly the more skilled and better-paid layers. The more oppressed majority of the working class is drawn only episodically into the struggle, during a period of exceptional upsurges in the labour movement. During such moments it is necessary to create organisations *ad hoc*, embracing the whole fighting mass: strike committees, factory committees, and finally, soviets.

(c) As organisations expressive of the top layers of the proletariat, trade unions, as witnessed by all past historical experience, including the fresh experience of the anarcho-syndicalist unions in Spain, developed powerful tendencies toward compromise with the bourgeois-democratic regime. In periods of acute class struggle, the leading bodies of the trade unions aim to become masters of the mass movement in order to render it harmless. This is already occurring during the period of simple strikes, especially in the case of the mass sit-down strikes which shake the principle of bourgeois property. In time of war or revolution, when the bourgeoisie is plunged into exceptional difficulties, trade union leaders usually become bourgeois ministers.

Therefore, the sections of the Fourth International should always strive not only to renew the top leadership of the trade unions, boldly and resolutely in critical moments advancing new militant leaders in place of routine functionaries and careerists, but also to create in all possible instances independent militant organisations corresponding more closely to the tasks of mass struggle against bourgeois society; and, if necessary, not flinching even in the face of a direct break with the conservative apparatus of the trade unions. If it be criminal to turn one's back on mass organisations for the sake of fostering sectarian factions, it is no less so passively to tolerate subordination of the revolutionary mass movement to the control of openly reactionary or disguised conservative ("progressive") bureaucratic cliques. Trade unions are not ends in themselves; they are but means along the road to proletarian revolution.

Factory Committees

During a transitional epoch, the workers' movement does not have a systematic and well-balanced, but a feverish and explosive character. Slogans as well as organisational forms should be subordinated to the indices of the movement. On guard against routine handling of a situation as against a plague, the leadership should respond sensitively to the initiative of the general population.

Sit-down strikes, the latest expression of this kind of initiative, go beyond the limits of "normal" capitalist procedure. Independently of the demands of the strikers, the temporary seizure of factories deals a blow to the idol, capitalist property. Every sit-down strike poses in a practical manner the question of who is boss of the factory: the capitalist or the workers?

If the sit-down strike raises this question episodically, the *factory committee* gives it organised expression. Elected by all the factory employees, the factory committee immediately creates a counterweight to the will of the administration.

To the reformist criticism of bosses of the so-called "economic royalist" type like Ford in contradistinction to "good," "democratic" exploiters, we counterpose the slogan of factory committees as centres of struggle against both the first and the second.

Trade union bureaucrats will, as a general rule, resist the creation of factory committees, just as they resist every bold step along the road of mobilising the general population.

However, the wider the sweep of the movement, the easier will it be to break this resistance. Where the closed shop has already been instituted in "peaceful" times, the committee will formally coincide with the usual organ of the trade union, but will renew its personnel and widen its functions. The prime significance of the committee, however, lies in the fact that it becomes the militant staff for such working class layers, as the trade union is usually incapable of moving to action. It is precisely from these more oppressed layers that the most self-sacrificing battalions of the revolution will come.

From the moment that the committee makes its appearance, a factual dual power is established in the factory. By its very essence it represents the transitional state, because it includes in itself two irreconcilable regimes: the capitalist and the proletarian. The fundamental significance of factory committees is precisely contained in the fact that they open the doors, if not to a direct revolutionary, then to a pre-Revolutionary period - between the bourgeois and the proletarian regimes. That the propagation of the factory committee idea is neither premature nor artificial is amply attested to by the waves of sit-down strikes spreading through several countries. New waves of this type will be inevitable in the immediate future. It is necessary to begin a campaign in favour of factory committees in time in order not to be caught unawares.

"Business Secrets" and Workers' Control of Industry

Liberal capitalism, based upon competition and free trade, has completely receded into the past. its successor, monopolistic capitalism not only does not mitigate the anarchy of the market, but on the contrary imparts to it a particularly convulsive character. The necessity of "controlling" economy, of placing state "guidance" over industry and of "planning" is today recognised—at least in words—by almost all current bourgeois and petty bourgeois tendencies, from fascist to Social Democratic. with the fascists, it is manly a question of "planned" plundering of the people for military purposes. The Social Democrats prepare to drain the ocean of anarchy with spoonfuls of bureaucratic "planning." Engineers and professors write articles about "technocracy." In their cowardly experiments in "regulation," democratic governments run head-on into the invincible sabotage of big capital.

The actual relationship existing between the exploiters and the democratic "controllers" is best characterised by the fact that the gentlemen "reformers" stop short in pious trepidation before the threshold of the trusts and their business "secrets." Here the principle of "non-interference" with business dominates. The accounts kept between the individual capitalist and society remain the secret of the capitalist: they are not the concern of society. The motivation offered for the principle of business "secrets" is ostensibly, as in the epoch of liberal capitalism, that of free ' competition." In reality, the trusts keep no secrets from one another. The business secrets of the present epoch are part of a persistent plot of monopoly capitalism against the interests of society. Projects for limiting the autocracy of "economic royalists" will continue to be pathetic farces as long as private owners of the social means of production can hide from producers and consumers the machinations of exploitation, robbery and fraud. The abolition of "business secrets" is the first step toward actual control of industry.

Workers no less than capitalists have the right to know the "secrets" of the factory, of the trust, of the whole branch of industry, of the national economy as a whole. First and foremost, banks, heavy industry and centralised transport should be placed under an observation glass.

The immediate tasks of workers' control should be to explain the debits and credits of society, beginning with individual business undertakings; to determine the actual share of the national income appropriated by individual capitalists and by the exploiters as a whole; to expose the behind-the-scenes deals and swindles of banks and trusts; finally, to reveal to all members of society that unconscionable squandering of human labour which is the result of capitalist anarchy and the naked pursuit of profits.

No office holder of the bourgeois state is in a position to carry out this work, no matter with how great authority one would wish to endow him. All the world was witness to the impotence of President Roosevelt and Premier Blum against the plottings of the "60" or "200 Families" of their respective nations. To break the resistance of the exploiters, the mass pressure of the proletariat is necessary. Only factory committees can bring about real control of production, calling in—as consultants but not as "technocrats"—specialists sincerely devoted to the people: accountants, statisticians, engineers, scientists, etc.

> To this very day, politicians of all stripes will claim they cannot "interfere" with business. If unions strike for higher pay, the police go in mob-handed. When bankers sabotage the economy they are punished

with bonuses. - DM

The struggle against unemployment is not to be considered without the calling for a broad and bold organisation of *public works.* But public works can have a continuous and progressive significance for society, as for the unemployed themselves, only when they are made part of a general plan worked out to cover a considerable number of years. Within the framework of this plan, the workers would demand resumption, as public utilities, of work in private businesses closed as a result of the crisis. Workers' control in such case: would be replaced by direct workers' management.

The working out of even the most elementary economic plan—from the point of view of the exploited, not the exploiters—is impossible without workers' control, that is, without the penetration of the workers' eye into all open and concealed springs of capitalist economy. Committees representing individual business enterprises should meet at conference to choose corresponding committees of trusts, whole branches of industry, economic regions and finally, of national industry as a whole. Thus, workers' control becomes a *school for planned economy*. On the basis of the experience of control, the proletariat will prepare itself for direct management of nationalised industry when the hour for that eventuality strikes.

To those capitalists, mainly of the lower and middle strata, who of their own accord sometimes offer to throw open their books to the workers — usually to demonstrate the necessity of lowering wages—the workers answer that they are not interested in the bookkeeping of individual bankrupts or semi-bankrupts but in the account ledgers of all exploiters as a whole. The workers cannot and do not wish to accommodate the level of their living conditions to the exigencies of individual capitalists, themselves victims of their own regime. The task is one of reorganising the whole system of production and distribution on a more dignified and workable basis if the abolition of business secrets be a necessary condition to workers' control, then control is the first step along the road to the socialist guidance of economy.

> **A scandal of the 1930s was the repeated attacks on the unemployed whose dole was depicted as the cause of the crisis. "Make the lazy swine work for their dole!" screamed the Daily Mail. Ring any bells? - DM**

Expropriation of Separate Groups of Capitalists

The socialist program of expropriation, i.e., of political overthrow of the bourgeoisie and liquidation of its economic domination, should in no case during the present transitional period hinder us from advancing, when the occasion warrants, the demand for the expropriation of several key branches of industry vital for national existence or of the most parasitic group of the bourgeoisie.

Thus, in answer to the pathetic jeremiads of the gentlemen democrats anent the dictatorship of the "60 Families" of the United States or the "200 Families" of France, we counterpose the demand for the expropriation of those 60 or 200 feudalistic capitalist overlords.

In precisely the same way, we demand the expropriation of the corporations holding monopolies on war industries, railroads, the most important sources of raw materials, etc.

The difference between these demands and the muddleheaded reformist slogan of "nationalisation" lies in the following: (1) we reject indemnification; (2) we warn the masses against demagogues of the People's Front who, giving lip service to nationalisation, remain in reality agents of capital; (3) we call upon the masses to rely only upon their own revolutionary strength; (4) we link up the question of expropriation with that of seizure of power by the workers and farmers.

The necessity of advancing the slogan of expropriation in the course of daily *agitation* in partial form, and not only in our propaganda in its more comprehensive aspects, is dictated by the fact that different branches of industry are on different levels of development, occupy a different place in the life of society, and pass through different stages of the class struggle. Only a general revolutionary upsurge of the proletariat can place the complete expropriation of the bourgeoisie on the order of the day. The task of transitional demands is to prepare the proletariat to solve this problem.

Expropriation of the Private Banks and State-ization of the Credit System

Imperialism means the domination of *finance capital*. Side by side with the trusts and syndicates, and very frequently rising above them, the banks concentrate in their hands the actual command over the economy. In their structure the banks express in a concentrated form the entire structure of modern capital: they combine tendencies of *monopoly* with tendencies of *anarchy*. They organise the miracles of technology, giant enterprises, mighty trusts; and they also organise high prices, crises and unemployment. It is impossible to take a single serious step in the struggle against monopolistic despotism and capitalistic anarchy—which supplement one another in their work of destruction—if the commanding posts of banks are left in the hands of predatory capitalists. In order to create a unified system of investments and credits, along a rational plan corresponding to the interests of the entire people, it is necessary to merge all the banks into a single national institution. Only the expropriation of the private banks and the concentration of the entire credit system in the hands of the state will provide the latter with the necessary actual, i.e., material resources—and not merely paper and bureaucratic resources — for economic planning.

The expropriation of the banks in no case implies the expropriation of bank deposits. On the contrary, the single *state bank* will be able to create much more favourable conditions for the small depositors than could the private banks. In the same way, only the state bank can establish for farmers, tradesmen and small merchants conditions of favourable, that is, cheap credit. Even more important, however, is the circumstance that the entire economy—first and foremost large-scale industry and transport directed by a single financial staff, will serve the vital interests of the workers and all other toilers.

However, the *state-ization of the banks* will produce these favourable results only if the state power itself passes completely from the hands of the exploiters into the hands of the toilers.

> **How prophetic is that final remark! We now know that nationalisation of the banks (RBS) can be used to prop up the system not to cleanse it of parasites. - DM**

The Picket Line, Defence Guards/Workers' Militia and The Arming of the Proletariat

Sit-down strikes are a serious warning from the masses addressed not only to the bourgeoisie but also to the organisations of the workers, including the Fourth International. In 1919-20, the Italian workers seized factories on their own initiative, thus signalling the news to their "leaders" of the coming of the social revolution. The "leaders" paid no heed to the signal. The victory of fascism was the result.

Sit down strikes do not yet mean the seizure of factories in the Italian manner, but they are a decisive step toward such seizures. The present crisis can sharpen the class struggle to an extreme point and bring nearer the moment of denouement. But that does not mean that a revolutionary situation comes on at one stroke. Actually, its approach is signalised by a continuous series of convulsions. One of these is the wave of sit-down strikes. The problem of the sections of the Fourth International is to help the proletarian vanguard understand the general character and tempo of our epoch and to fructify in time the struggle of the masses with ever more resolute and organisational measures.

The sharpening of the proletariat's struggle means the sharpening of the methods of counterattack on the part of capital. New waves of sit down strikes can call forth and undoubtedly will call forth resolute countermeasures on the part of the bourgeoisie. Preparatory work is already being done by the confidential staffs of big trusts. Woe to the revolutionary organisations, woe to the proletariat if it is again caught unawares!

The bourgeoisie is nowhere satisfied with the official police and army. In the United States even during "peaceful" times the bourgeoisie maintains militarised battalions of scabs and privately armed thugs in factories. To this must now be added the various groups of American Nazis. The French bourgeoisie at the first approach of danger mobilised semi-legal and illegal fascist detachments, including such as are in the army. No sooner does the pressure of the English workers once again become stronger than immediately the fascist bands are doubled, trebled, increased tenfold to come out in bloody march against the workers. The bourgeoisie keeps itself most accurately informed about the fact that in the present epoch the class struggle irresistibly tends to transform itself into civil war. The examples of Italy, Germany, Austria, Spain and other countries taught considerably more to the magnates and lackeys of capital than to the official leaders of the proletariat.

The politicians of the Second and Third Internationals as well as the bureaucrats of the trade unions, consciously close their eyes to the bourgeoisie's private army; otherwise they could not preserve their alliance with it for even twenty-four hours. The reformists systematically implant in the minds of the workers the notion that the sacredness of democracy is best guaranteed when the bourgeoisie is armed to the teeth and the workers are unarmed.

The duty of the Fourth International is to put an end to such slavish polices once and for all. The petty bourgeois democrats—including Social Democrats, Stalinists and Anarchists—yell louder about the struggle against fascism the more cravenly they capitulate to it in actuality. Only armed workers' detachments, who feel the support of tens of millions of toilers behind them, can successfully prevail against the fascist bands. The struggle against fascism does not start in the liberal editorial office but in the factory—and ends in the street. Scabs and private gunmen in factory plants are the basic nuclei of the fascist army. *Strike pickets* are the basic nuclei of the proletarian army. This is our point of departure. In connection with every strike and street demonstration, it is imperative to propagate the necessity of creating *workers' groups for self-defence*. It is necessary to write this slogan into the program of the revolutionary wing of the trade unions. It is imperative wherever possible, beginning with the youth groups, to organise groups for self-defence, to drill and acquaint them with the use of arms.

A new upsurge of the mass movement should serve not only to increase the number of these units but also to unite them according to neighbourhoods, cities, regions. It is necessary to give organised expression to the valid hatred of the workers toward scabs and bands of gangsters and fascists. It is necessary to advance the slogan of a *workers' militia* as the one Serious guarantee for the inviolability of workers' organisations, meetings and press.

Only with the help of such systematic, persistent, indefatigable, courageous agitational and organisational work always on the basis of the experience of the general population themselves, is it possible to root out from their consciousness the traditions of submissiveness and passivity; to train detachments of heroic fighters capable of setting an example to all toilers; to inflict a series of tactical defeats upon the armed thugs of counterrevolution; to raise the self-confidence of the exploited and oppressed; to compromise Fascism in the eyes of the petty bourgeoisie and pave the road for the conquest of power by the proletariat.

Engels defined the state as "bodies of armed men." *The arming of the proletariat* is an imperative concomitant element to its struggle for liberation. When the proletariat wills it, it will find the road and the means to arming. In this field, also, else leadership falls naturally to the sections of the Fourth International.

This seems a far cry from the present situation in the UK. In the 1930s, fascist gangs threatened the workers' movement. Yet of course the economic crists sharpens class antagonism and it is possible those days could come again. Be prepared as the boy scouts say!

The Alliance of the Workers and Farmers

The brother-in-arms and counterpart of the worker in the country is the agricultural labourer. They are two parts of one and the same class. Their interests are inseparable. The industrial workers' program of transitional demands, with changes here and there, is likewise the program of the agricultural proletariat.

The peasants (farmers) represent another class: they are the petty bourgeoisie of the village. The petty bourgeoisie is made up of various layers, from the semi-proletarian to the exploiter elements. In accordance with this, the political task of the industrial proletariat is to carry the class struggle into the country. Only thus will he be able to draw a dividing line between his allies and his enemies.

The peculiarities of national development of each country find their queerest expression in the status of farmers and, to some extent, of the urban petty bourgeoisie (artisans and shopkeepers). These classes, no matter how numerically strong they may be, essentially are representative survivals of pre-capitalist forms of production. The sections of the Fourth International should work out with all possible concreteness a program of transitional demands concerning the peasants (farmers) and urban petty bourgeoisie, in conformity with the conditions of each country. The advanced workers should learn to give clear and concrete answers to the questions put by their future allies.

While the farmer remains an "independent" petty producer he is in need of cheap credit, of agricultural machines and fertiliser at prices he can afford to pay, favourable conditions of transport, and conscientious organisation of the market for his agricultural products. But the banks, the trusts, the merchants rob the farmer from every side. Only the farmers themselves with the help of the workers can curb this robbery. *Committees elected by small farmers* should make their appearance on the national scene and jointly with the workers' committees and committees of bank employees take into their hands control off transport, credit, and mercantile operations affecting agriculture.

By falsely citing the "excessive" demands of the workers the big bourgeoisie skilfully transforms the question of *commodity prices* into a wedge to be driven between the workers and farmers and between the workers and the petty bourgeoisie of the cities. The peasant, artisan, small merchant, unlike the industrial worker, office and civil service employee, cannot demand a wage increase corresponding to the increase in prices. The official struggle of the government with high prices is only a deception of the general population. But the farmers, artisans, merchants, in their capacity of consumers, can step into the politics of price-fixing shoulder to shoulder with the workers. To the capitalist's lamentations about costs of production, of transport and trade, the consumers answer: "Show us your books; we demand control over the fixing of prices." The organs of this control should be the *committees on prices*, made up of delegates from the factories, trade unions, co-operatives, farmers' organisations, the "little man" of the city, housewives, etc. By this means the workers will be able to prove to the farmers that the real reason for high prices is not high wages but the exorbitant profits of the capitalists and the overhead expenses of capitalist anarchy.

The program for the *nationalisation of the land and collectivisation of agriculture* should be so drawn that from its very basis it should exclude the possibility of expropriation of small farmers and their compulsory collectivisation. The farmer will remain owner of his plot of land as long as he himself believes it possible or necessary. In order to rehabilitate the program of socialism in the eyes of the farmer, it is necessary to expose mercilessly the Stalinist methods of collectivisation, which are dictated not by the interests of the farmers or workers but by the interests of the bureaucracy.

The expropriation of the expropriators likewise does not signify forcible confiscation of the property of artisans and shopkeepers. On the contrary, workers' control of banks and trusts—even more, the nationalisation of these concerns, can create for the urban petty bourgeoisie incomparably more favourable conditions of credit purchase, and sale than is possible under the unchecked domination of the monopolies. Dependence upon private capital will be replaced by dependence upon the state, which will be the more attentive to the needs of its small co-workers and agents the more firmly the toilers themselves keep the state in their own hands .

The practical participation of the exploited farmers in the control of different fields of economy will allow them to decide for themselves whether or not it would be profitable for them to go over to collective working of the land—at what date and on what scale. Industrial workers should consider themselves duty-bound to show farmers every co-operation in travelling this road: through the trade unions, factory committees, and, above all, through a workers' and farmers' government.

The alliance proposed by the proletariat—not to the "middle classes in general but to the exploited layers of the urban and rural petty bourgeoisie, against all exploiters, including those of the "middle classes"—can be based not on compulsion but only on free consent, which should be consolidated in a special "contract." This "contract" is the program of transitional demands voluntarily accepted by both sides.

The Struggle Against Imperialism and War

The whole world outlook, and consequently also the inner political life of individual countries, is overcast by the threat of world war. Already the imminent catastrophe sends violent ripples of apprehension through the very broadest masses of mankind.

The Second International repeats its infamous politics of 1914 with all the greater assurance since today it is the Comintern which plays first fiddle in chauvinism. As quickly as the danger of war assumed concrete outline the Stalinists, outstripping the bourgeois and petty bourgeois pacifists by far, became blatant haranguers for so-called "national defence." The revolutionary struggle against war thus rests fully on the shoulders of the Fourth International.

The Bolshevik-Leninist policy regarding this question, formulated in the thesis of the International Secretariat (*War and the Fourth International*, 1934), preserves all of its force today.

In the next period a revolutionary party will depend for success primarily on its policy on the question of war. A correct policy is composed of two elements: an uncompromising attitude on imperialism and its wars, and the ability to base one's program on the experience of the general population themselves.

The bourgeoisie and its agents use the war question, more than any other, to deceive the people by means of abstractions, general formulas, lame phraseology: "neutrality," "collective defence," "arming for the defence of peace," "struggle against fascism," and so on. All such formulas reduce themselves in the end to the fact that the war question, i.e., the fate of the people, is left in the hands of the imperialists, their governing staffs, their diplomacy, their generals, with all their intrigues and plots against the people.

The Fourth International rejects with abhorrence all such abstractions which play the same role in the democratic camp as in the fascist: "honour " "blood," "race." But abhorrence is not enough. It is imperative to help the masses discern, by means of verifying criteria, slogans and demands, the concrete essence of fraudulent abstractions.

"*Disarmament?*"—But the entire question revolves around who will disarm whom. The only disarmament which can avert or end war is the disarmament of the bourgeoisie by the workers. But to disarm the bourgeoisie, the workers must arm themselves.

"*Neutrality?*"—But the proletariat is nothing like neutral in the war between Japan and China, or a war between Germany and the USSR. "Then what is meant Is the defence of China and the USSR?" Of course! But not by the imperialists who will strangle both China and the USSR.

"*Defence of the Fatherland?*"—But by this abstraction, the bourgeoisie understands the defence of its profits and plunder. We stand ready to defend the fatherland from foreign capitalists, if we first bind our own (capitalists) hand and foot and hinder them from attacking foreign fatherlands; if the workers and the farmers of our country become its real masters, if the wealth of the country be transferred from the hands of a tiny minority to the hands of the people; if the army becomes a weapon of the exploited instead of the exploiters.

It is necessary to interpret these fundamental ideas by breaking them up into more concrete and partial ones, dependent upon the course of events and the orientation of thought of the masses. In addition, it is necessary to differentiate strictly between the pacifism of the diplomat, professor, journalist, and the pacifism of the carpenter, agricultural worker, and the charwoman. In one case, pacifism is a screen for imperialism; in the other, it is the confused expression of distrust in imperialism. When the small farmer or worker speaks about the defence of the fatherland, he means defence of his home, his family and other similar families from invasion, bombs and poison gas. The capitalist and his journalist understand by the defence of the fatherland the seizure of colonies and markets, the predatory increase of the "national" share of world income. Bourgeois pacifism and patriotism are shot through with deceit. In the pacifism and even patriotism of the oppressed, there are elements which reflect on the one hand a hatred of destructive war, and on the other a clinging to what they believe to be their own good—elements which we must know how to seize upon in order to draw the requisite conclusions.

Using these considerations as its point of departure, the Fourth International supports every, even if insufficient, demand, if it can draw the masses to a certain extent into active polities, awaken their criticism and strengthen their control over the machinations of the bourgeoisie.

From this point of view, our American section, for example, entirely supports the proposal for establishing a referendum on the question of declaring war. No democratic reform, it is understood, can by itself prevent the rulers from provoking war when they wish it. It is necessary to give frank warning of this. But not withstanding the illusions of the masses in regard to the proposed referendum, their support of it reflects the distrust felt by workers and farmers for bourgeois government and Congress. Without supporting and without sparing illusions, it is necessary to support with all possible strength the progressive distrust of the exploited toward the exploiters. The more widespread the movement for the referendum becomes, the sooner will the bourgeois pacifists move away from it; the more completely will the betrayers of the Comintern be compromised; the more acute will distrust of the imperialists become.

From this viewpoint, it is necessary to advance the demand: electoral rights for men and women beginning with age of 18. Those who will be called upon to die for the fatherland tomorrow should have the right to vote today. The struggle against war must first of all begin with the *revolutionary mobilisation of the youth*.

Light must be shed upon the problem of war from all angles, hinging upon the side from which it will confront the masses at a given moment.

War is a gigantic commercial enterprise, especially for the war industry. The "60 Families" are therefore first-line patriots and the chief provocateurs of war. *Workers' control of war industries* is the first step in the struggle against the "manufacturers" of war.

To the slogan of the reformists: *a tax on military profit*, we counterpose the slogans: *confiscation of military profit* and *expropriation of the traffickers in war industries*. Where military industry is "nationalised," as in France, the slogan of *workers' control* preserves its full strength. The proletariat has as little confidence in the government of the bourgeoisie as in an individual capitalist

Not one man and not one penny for the bourgeois government!

Not an armaments program but a program of useful public works!

Complete independence of workers' organisations from military-police control!

Once and for all we must tear from the hands of the greedy and merciless imperialist clique, scheming behind the backs of the people, the disposition of the people's fate. In accordance with this, we demand:

> Complete abolition of secret diplomacy; all treaties and agreements to be made accessible to all workers and farmers; Military training and arming of workers and farmers under direct control of workers' and farmers' committees; Creation of military schools for the training of commanders among the toilers, chosen by workers' organisations; Substitution for the standing army of a *people's militia*, indissolubly linked up with factories, mines, farms, etc.

Imperialist war is the continuation and sharpening of the predatory politics of the bourgeoisie. The struggle of the proletariat against war is the continuation and sharpening of its class struggle. The beginning of war alters the situation and partially the means of struggle between the classes, but not the aim and basic course. The imperialist bourgeoisie dominates the world. In its basic character the approaching war will therefore be an imperialist war. The fundamental content of the politics of the international proletariat will consequently be a struggle against imperialism and its war. In this struggle the basic principle is: "the chief enemy is in *your own* country" or "the defeat of *your own* (imperialist) government is the lesser evil."

But not all countries of the world are imperialist countries. On the contrary, the majority are victims of imperialism. Some of the colonial or semi colonial countries will undoubtedly attempt to utilise the war in order to east off the yoke of slavery. Their war will be not imperialist but liberating. It will be the duty of the international proletariat to aid the oppressed countries in their war against oppressors. The same duty applies in regard to aiding the USSR, or whatever other workers' government might arise before the war or during the war. The defeat of *every* imperialist government in the struggle with the workers' state or with a colonial country is the lesser evil.

The workers of imperialist countries, however, cannot help an anti-imperialist country through their own government, no matter what might be the diplomatic and military relations between the two countries at a given moment. If the governments find themselves in a temporary and, by the very essence of the matter, unreliable alliance, then the proletariat of the imperialist country continues to remain in class opposition to its own government and supports the non-imperialist "ally" through its *own* methods, i.e., through the methods of the international class struggle (agitation not only against their perfidious allies, but also in favour of a workers' state in a colonial country; boycott, strikes, in one case; rejection of boycott and strikes in another case, etc.)

In supporting the colonial country or the USSR in a war, the proletariat does not in the slightest degree solidarise either with the bourgeois government of the colonial country or with the Thermidorian bureaucracy of the USSR. On the contrary, it maintains full political independence from the one as from the other. Giving aid in a just and progressive war, the revolutionary proletariat wins the sympathy of the workers in the colonies and in the USSR, strengthens there the authority and influence of the Fourth International, and increases its ability to help overthrow the bourgeois government in the colonial country, the reactionary bureaucracy in the USSR.

At the beginning of the war the sections of the Fourth International will inevitably feel themselves isolated: every war takes the national masses unawares and impels them to the side of the government apparatus. The internationalists will have to swim against the stream. However, the devastation and misery brought about by the new war, which in the first months will far outstrip the bloody horrors of 1914-18. will quickly prove sobering The discontents of the masses and their revolt will grow by leaps and bounds. The sections of the Fourth International will be found at the head of the revolutionary tide. The program of transitional demands will gain burning actuality. The problem of the conquest of power by the proletariat will loom in full stature.

Before exhausting or drowning mankind in blood, capitalism befouls the world atmosphere with the poisonous vapours of national and race hatred. *Anti-Semitism* today is one of the most malignant convulsions of capitalism's death agony.

An uncompromising disclosure of the roots of race prejudice and all forms and shades of national arrogance and chauvinism, particularly anti Semitism, should become part of the daily work of all sections of the Fourth International, as the most important part of the struggle against imperialism and war. Our basic slogan remains: Workers of the World Unite!

Workers' and Farmers' Government

This formula, "workers' and farmers' government," first appeared in the agitation of the Bolsheviks in 1917 and was definitely accepted after the October Revolution. In the final instance it represented nothing more than the popular designation for the already established dictatorship of the proletariat. The significance of this designation comes mainly from the that it underscored the idea of an *alliance between the proletariat and the peasantry* upon which the Soviet power rests.

When the Comintern of the epigones tried to revive the formula buried by history of the "democratic dictatorship of the proletariat and peasantry," it gave to the formula of the "workers' and peasants' government" a completely different, purely "democratic," i.e., bourgeois content, *counterposing* it to the dictatorship of the proletariat. The Bolshevik-Leninists resolutely rejected the slogan of the "workers' and peasants' government" in the bourgeois-democratic version. They affirmed then and affirm now that. when the party of the proletariat refuses to step beyond bourgeois democratic limits, its alliance with the peasantry is simply turned into a support for capital, as was the ease with the Mensheviks and the Social Revolutionaries in 1917, with the Chinese Communist Party in 1925-27, and as is now the ease with the "People's Front" in Spain, France and other countries.

From April to September 1917, the Bolsheviks demanded that the S.R.s and Mensheviks break with the liberal bourgeoisie and take power into their own hands. Under this provision the Bolshevik Party promised the Mensheviks an the S.R.s, as the petty bourgeois representatives of the worker and peasants, its revolutionary aid against the bourgeoisie categorically refusing, however, either to enter into the government of the Mensheviks and S.R.s or to carry political responsibility for it. If the Mensheviks and S.R.s had actually broke with the Cadets (liberals) and with foreign imperialism, then the "workers' and peasants' government" created by them could only have hastened and facilitated the establishment of the dictatorship of the proletariat. But it was exactly because of this that the leadership of petty bourgeois democracy resisted with all possible strength the establishment of its own government. The experience of Russia demonstrated, and the experience of Spain and France once again confirms, that even under very favourable conditions the parties of petty bourgeois democracy (S.R.s, Social Democrats, Stalinists, Anarchists) are incapable of creating a government of workers and peasants, that is, a government independent of the bourgeoisie.

Nevertheless, the demand of the Bolsheviks, addressed to the Mensheviks and the S.R.s: "Break with the bourgeoisie, take the power into your own hands!" had for the masses tremendous educational significance. The obstinate unwillingness of the Mensheviks and S.R.s to take power, so dramatically exposed during the July Days, definitely doomed them before mass opinion and prepared the victory of the Bolsheviks.

The central task of the Fourth International consists in freeing the proletariat from the old leadership, whose conservatism is in complete contradiction to the catastrophic eruptions of disintegrating capitalism and represents the chief obstacle to historical progress. The chief accusation which the Fourth International advances against the traditional organisations of the proletariat is the fact that they do not wish to tear themselves away from the political semi-corpse of the bourgeoisie. Under these conditions the demand, systematically addressed to the old leadership: "Break with the bourgeoisie, take the power!" is an extremely important weapon for exposing the treacherous character of the parties and organisations of the Second, Third and Amsterdam Internationals. The slogan, "workers' and farmers' government," is thus acceptable to us only in the sense that it had in 1917 with the Bolsheviks, i.e., as an anti-bourgeois and anti-capitalist slogan. but in no case in that "democratic" sense which later the epigones gave it, transforming it from a bridge to Socialist revolution into the chief barrier upon its path.

Of all parties and organisations which base themselves on the workers and peasants and speak in their name, we demand that they break politically from the bourgeoisie and enter upon the road of struggle for the workers' and farmers' government. On this road we promise them full support against capitalist reaction. At the same time, we indefatigably develop agitation around those transitional demands which should in our opinion form the program of the "workers' and farmers' government."

Is the creation of such a government by the traditional workers' organisations possible? Past experience shows, as has already been stated, that this is, to say the least, highly improbable. However, one cannot categorically deny in advance the theoretical possibility that, under the influence of completely exceptional circumstances (war, defeat, financial crash, mass revolutionary pressure, etc.), the petty bourgeois parties, including the Stalinists, may go further than they wish along the road to a break with the bourgeoisie. In any case one thing is not to be doubted: even if this highly improbable variant somewhere at some time becomes a reality and the "workers' and farmers' government" in the above-mentioned sense is established in fact, it would represent merely a short episode on the road to the actual dictatorship of the proletariat.

However, there is no need to indulge in guesswork. The agitation around the slogan of a workers'-farmers' government preserves under all conditions a tremendous educational value. And not accidentally. This generalised slogan proceeds entirely along the line of the political development of our epoch (the bankruptcy and decomposition of the old bourgeois parties, the downfall of democracy, the growth of fascism, the accelerated drive of the workers toward more active and aggressive politics). Each of the transitional demands should, therefore, lead to one and the same political conclusion: the workers need to break with all traditional parties of the bourgeoisie in order, jointly with the farmers, to establish their own power.

It is impossible in advance to foresee what will be the concrete stages of the revolutionary mobilisation of the masses. The sections of the Fourth International should critically orient themselves at each new stage and advance such slogans as will aid the striving of the workers for independent politics, deepen the class struggle of these politics, destroy reformist and pacifist illusions, strengthen the connection of the vanguard with the masses, and prepare the revolutionary conquest of power.

Soviets

Factory committees, as already stated, are elements of dual power inside the factory. Consequently, their existence is possible only under conditions of increasing pressure by the masses. This is likewise true of special mass groupings for the struggle *against war*, of the *committees on prices*, and all other new centres of the movement, the very appearance of which bears witness to the fact that the class struggle has overflowed the limits of the traditional organisations of the proletariat.

These new organs and centres, however, will soon begin to feel their lack of cohesion and their insufficiency. Not one of the transitional demands can be fully met under the conditions of preserving the bourgeois regime. At the same time, the deepening of the social crisis will increase not only the sufferings of the masses but also their impatience, persistence and pressure. Ever new layers of the oppressed will raise their heads and come forward with their demands. Millions of toil-worn "little men," to whom the reformist leaders never gave a thought, will begin to pound insistently on the doors of the workers' organisations. The unemployed will join the movement. The agricultural workers, the ruined and semi-ruined farmers, the oppressed of the cities, the women workers, housewives, proletarianised layers of the intelligentsia—all of these will seek unity and leadership.

How are the different demands and forms of struggle to be harmonised, even if only within the limits of one city? History has already answered this question: through *soviets*. These will unite the representatives of all the fighting groups. For this purpose, no one has yet proposed a different form of organisation; indeed, it would hardly be possible to think up a better one. Soviets are not limited to an *a priori* party program. They throw open their doors to all the exploited. Through these doors pass representatives of all strata, drawn into the general current of the struggle. The organisation, broadening out together with the movement, is renewed again and again in its womb. All political currents of the proletariat can struggle for leadership of the soviets on the basis of the widest democracy. The slogan of *soviets*, therefore, crowns the program of transitional demands.

Soviets can arise only at the time when the mass movement enters into an openly revolutionary stage. From the first moment of their appearance, the soviets, acting as a pivot around which millions of toilers are united in their struggle against the exploiters, become competitors and opponents of local authorities and then of the central government. If the factory committee creates a dual power in the factory, then the soviets initiate a period of dual power in the country.

Dual power in its turn is the culminating point of the transitional period. Two regimes, the bourgeois and the proletarian, are irreconcilably opposed to each other. Conflict between them is inevitable. The fate of society depends on the outcome. Should the revolution be defeated, the fascist dictatorship of the bourgeoisie will follow. In the case of victory, the power of the soviets, that is, the dictatorship of the proletariat and the socialist reconstruction of society, will arise.

Backward Countries and the Program of Transitional Demands

Colonial and semi-colonial countries are backward countries by their very essence. But backward countries are part of a world dominated by imperialism. Their development, therefore, has a *combined* character: the most primitive economic forms are combined with the last word in capitalist technique and culture. In like manner are defined the political strivings of the proletariat of backward countries: the struggle for the most elementary achievements of national independence and bourgeois democracy is combined with the socialist struggle against world imperialism. Democratic slogans, transitional demands and the problems of the socialist revolution are not divided into separate historical epochs in this struggle, but stem directly from one another. The Chinese proletariat had barely begun to organise trade unions before it had to provide for soviets. In this sense, the present program is completely applicable to colonial and semi colonial countries, at least to those where the proletariat has become capable of carrying on independent politics.

The central task of the colonial and semi-colonial countries is the *agrarian revolution*, i.e., liquidation of feudal heritages, and *national independence*, i.e., the overthrow of the imperialist yoke. Both tasks are closely linked with each other.

It is impossible merely to reject the democratic program; it is imperative that in the struggle the masses outgrow it. The slogan for a National (or Constituent) Assembly preserves its full force for such countries as China or India. This slogan must be indissolubly tied up with the problem of national liberation and agrarian reform. As a primary step, the workers must be armed with this democratic program. Only they will be able to summon and unite the farmers. On the basis of the revolutionary democratic program, it is necessary to oppose the workers to the "national" bourgeoisie. Then, at a certain stage in the mobilisation of the masses under the slogans of revolutionary democracy, soviets can and should arise. Their historical role in each given period, particularly their relation to the National Assembly, will be determined by the political level of the proletariat, the bond between them and the peasantry, and the character of the proletarian party policies. Sooner or later, the soviets should overthrow bourgeois democracy. Only they are capable of bringing the democratic revolution to a conclusion and likewise opening an era of socialist revolution.

The relative weight of the individual democratic and transitional demands in the proletariat's struggle, their mutual ties and their order of presentation, is determined by the peculiarities and specific conditions of each backward country and to a considerable extent by the *degree* of its backwardness. Nevertheless, the general trend of revolutionary development in all backward countries can be determined by the formula of the permanent revolution in the sense definitely imparted to it by the three revolutions in Russia (1905, February 1917, October 1917).

The Comintern has provided backward countries with a classic example of how it is possible to ruin a powerful and promising revolution. During the stormy mass upsurge in China in 1925-27, the Comintern failed to advance the slogan for a National Assembly, and at the same time forbade the creation of soviets. (The bourgeois party, the Kuomintang, was to replace, according to Stalin's plan, both the National Assembly and soviets.) After the masses had been smashed by the Kuomintang, the Comintern organised a caricature of a soviet in Canton. Following the inevitable collapse of the Canton uprising, the Comintern took the road of guerrilla warfare a peasant soviets with complete passivity on the part of the industrial proletariat. Landing thus in a blind alley, the Comintern took advantage of the Sino-Japanese War to liquidate "Soviet China" with a stroke of the pen, subordinating not only the peasant "Red Army" but also the so-called "Communist" Party to the identical Kuomintang, i.e., the bourgeoisie.

Having betrayed the international proletarian revolution for the sake of friendship with the "democratic" slavemasters, the Comintern could not help betraying simultaneously also the struggle for liberation of the colonial masses, and, indeed, with even greater cynicism than did the Second International before it. One of the tasks of People's Front and "national defence" politics is to turn hundreds of millions of the colonial population into cannon fodder for "democratic" imperialism. The banner on which is emblazoned the struggle for the liberation of the colonial and semi colonial peoples, i.e., a good half of mankind, has definitely passed into the hands of the Fourth International.

The Program of Transitional Demands in Fascist Countries

It is a far cry today from the time when the strategists of the Comintern announced the victory of Hitler as being merely a step toward the victory of Thaelmann. Thaelmann has been in Hitler's prisons now for more than five years. Mussolini has held Italy enchained by fascism for more than sixteen years. Throughout this time, the parties of the Second and Third Internationals have been impotent, not only to conduct a mass movement, but even to create a serious illegal organisation, even to some extent comparable to the Russian revolutionary parties during the epoch of Tsarism.

Not the least reason exists for explaining these failures by reference to the power of fascist ideology. (Essentially, Mussolini never advanced any sort of ideology.) Hitler's "ideology" never seriously gripped the workers. Those layers of the population which at one time were intoxicated with fascism i.e., chiefly the middle classes, have had enough time in which to sober up. The fact that a somewhat perceptible opposition is limited to Protestant and Catholic church circles is not explained by the might of the semi-delirious and semi-charlatan theories of "race" and "blood," but by the terrific collapse of the ideologies of democracy, Social Democracy and the Comintern.

After the massacre of the Paris Commune, black reaction reigned for nearly eight years. After the defeat of the 1905 Russian revolution, the toiling masses remained in a stupor for almost as long a period. But in both instances the phenomenon was only one of physical defeat, conditioned by the relationship of forces. In Russia, in addition, it concerned an almost virgin proletariat. The Bolshevik faction had at that time not celebrated even its third birthday. It is completely otherwise in Germany where the leadership came from powerful parties one of which had existed for seventy years, the other almost fifteen. Both these parties, with millions of voters behind them, were morally paralysed before the battle and capitulated without a battle. History has recorded no parallel catastrophe. The German proletariat was not smashed by the enemy in battle. It was crushed by the cowardice, baseness, perfidy of its own parties. Small wonder then that it has lost faith in everything in which it had been accustomed to believe for almost three generations. Hitler's victory in turn strengthened Mussolini.

The protracted failure of revolutionary work in Spain or Germany is but the reward for the criminal politics of the Social Democracy and the Comintern. Illegal work needs not only the sympathy of the masses but the conscious enthusiasm of its advanced strata. But can enthusiasm possibly be expected for historically bankrupt organisations? The majority of those who come forth as émigré leaders are either demoralised to the very marrow of their bones, agents of the Kremlin and the GPU, or Social Democratic ex-ministers, who dream that the workers by some sort of miracle will return them to their lost posts. Is it possible to imagine even for a minute these gentlemen in the role of future leaders of the "anti-fascist" revolution?

And events on the world arena—the smashing of the Austrian workers, the defeat of the Spanish Revolution, the degeneration of the Soviet state — could not give aid to a revolutionary upsurge in Italy and Germany. Since for political information the German and Italian workers depend in great measure upon the radio, it is possible to say with assurance that the Moscow radio station, combining Thermidorian lies with stupidity and insolence, has become the most powerful factor in the demoralisation of the workers in the totalitarian states. In this respect as in others, Stalin acts merely as Goebbels' assistant.

At the same time, the class antagonisms which brought about the victory of fascism, continuing their work under fascism too, are gradually undermining it. The masses are more dissatisfied than ever. Hundreds and thousands of self-sacrificing workers, in spite of everything, continue to carry on revolutionary mole-work. A new generation, which has nor directly experienced the shattering of old traditions and high hopes, has come to the fore. Irresistibly, the molecular preparation of the proletarian revolution proceeds beneath the heavy totalitarian tombstone. But, for concealed energy to flare into open revolt, it is necessary that the vanguard of the proletariat find new perspectives, a new program and a new unblemished banner.

Herein lies the chief handicap. It is extremely difficult for workers in fascist countries to make a choice of a new program. A program is verified by experience. And it is precisely experience in mass movements which is lacking in countries of totalitarian despotism. It is very likely that a genuine proletarian success in one of the "democratic" countries will be necessary to give impetus to the revolutionary movement on fascist territory. A similar effect is possible by means of a financial or military catastrophe. At present, it is imperative that primarily propagandistic, preparatory work be carried on which will yield large-scale results only in the future. One thing can be stated with conviction even at this point: once it breaks through, the revolutionary wave in fascist countries will immediately be a grandiose sweep and under no circumstances will stop short at the experiment of resuscitating some sort of Weimar corpse.

It is from this point onward that an uncompromising divergence begins between the Fourth International and the old parties, which outlive their bankruptcy. The émigré "People's Front" is the most malignant and perfidious variety of all possible People's Fronts. Essentially, it signifies the impotent longing for coalition with a non-existent liberal bourgeoisie. Had it met with success, it would simply have prepared a series of new defeats of the Spanish type for the proletariat. A merciless exposure of the theory and practice of the "People's Front" is therefore the first condition for a revolutionary struggle against fascism.

Of course, this does not mean that the Fourth International rejects democratic slogans as a means of mobilising the masses against fascism. On the contrary, such slogans at certain moments can play a serious role. But the formulae of democracy (freedom of press, the right to unionise, etc.) mean for us only incidental or episodic slogans in the independent movement of the proletariat and not a democratic noose fastened to the neck of the proletariat by the bourgeoisie's agents (Spain!). As soon as the movement assumes something of a mass character, the democratic slogans will be intertwined with the transitional ones; factory committees, it may be supposed, will appear before the old routinists rush from their chancelleries to organise trade unions; soviets will cover Germany before a new Constituent Assembly will gather in Weimar. The same applies to Italy and the rest of the totalitarian and semi-totalitarian countries.

Fascism plunged these countries into political barbarism. But it did not change their social structure. Fascism is a tool in the hands of finance capital and not of feudal landowners. A revolutionary program should base itself on the dialectics of the class struggle, obligatory also to fascist countries, and not on the psychology of terrified bankrupts. The Fourth International rejects with disgust the ways of political masquerade which impelled the Stalinists, the former heroes of the "Third Period," to appear in turn behind the masks of Catholics, Protestants, Jews, German nationalists, liberals—only in order to hide their own unattractive face. The Fourth International always and everywhere appears under its own banner. It proposes its own program openly to the proletariat in fascist countries. The advanced workers of all the world are already firmly convinced that the overthrow of Mussolini, Hitler and their agents and imitators will occur only under the leadership of the Fourth International.

The USSR and Problems of the Transitional Epoch

The Soviet Union emerged from the October Revolution as a workers' state. State ownership of the means of production, a necessary prerequisite to socialist development, opened up the possibility of rapid growth of the productive forces. But the apparatus of the workers' state underwent a complete degeneration at the same time: it was transformed from a weapon of the working class into a weapon of bureaucratic violence against the working class and more and more a weapon for the sabotage of the country's economy. The bureaucratisation of a backward and isolated workers' state and the transformation of the bureaucracy into an all-powerful privileged caste constitute the most convincing refutation—not only theoretically, but this time, practically—of the theory of socialism in one country.

The USSR thus embodies terrific contradictions. But it still remains a *degenerated workers' state*. Such is the social diagnosis. The political prognosis has an alternative character: either the bureaucracy, becoming ever more the organ of the world bourgeoisie in the workers' state, will overthrow the new forms of property and plunge the country back to capitalism; or the working class will crush the bureaucracy and open the way to socialism.

To the sections of the Fourth International, the Moscow Trials came not as a surprise and not as a result of the personal madness of the Kremlin dictator, but as the legitimate offspring of the Thermidor. They grew out of the unbearable conflicts within the Soviet bureaucracy itself, which in turn mirror the contradictions between the bureaucracy and the people, as well as the deepening antagonisms among the "people" themselves. The bloody "fantastic" nature of the trials gives the measure of the intensity of the contradictions and by the same token predicts the approach of the denouement.

The public utterances of former foreign representatives of the Kremlin, who refused to return to Moscow, irrefutably confirm in their own way that all shades of political thought are to be found among the bureaucracy: from genuine Bolshevism (Ignace Reiss) to complete fascism (F. Butenko). The revolutionary elements within the bureaucracy, only a small minority, reflect, passively it is true, the socialist interests of the proletariat. The fascist, counterrevolutionary elements, growing uninterruptedly, express with even greater consistency the interests of world imperialism. These candidates for the role of compradors consider, not without reason, that the new ruling layer can insure their positions of privilege only through rejection of nationalisation, collectivisation and monopoly of foreign trade in the name of the assimilation of "Western civilisation." i.e., capitalism. Between these two poles, there are intermediate, diffused Menshevik-S.R.-liberal tendencies which gravitate toward bourgeois democracy.

Within the very ranks of that so-called "classless" society, there unquestionably exist groupings exactly similar to those in the bureaucracy, only less sharply expressed and in inverse proportions: conscious capitalist tendencies distinguish mainly the prosperous part of the collective farms *(kolkhozi)* and are characteristic of only a small minority of the population. But this layer provides itself with a wide base for petty bourgeois tendencies of accumulating personal wealth at the expense of general poverty, and are consciously encouraged by the bureaucracy.

Atop this system of mounting antagonisms, trespassing ever more on the social equilibrium, the Thermidorian oligarchy, today reduced mainly to Stalin's Bonapartist clique, hangs on by terrorist methods. The latest judicial frame-ups were aimed as a blow *against the left*.

This is true also of the mopping up of the leaders of the Right Opposition, because the Right group of the old Bolshevik Party, seen from the view point of the bureaucracy's interests and tendencies, represented a *left* danger. The fact that the Bonapartist clique, likewise in fear of its own right allies of the type of Butenko, is forced in the interests of self-preservation to execute the generation of Old Bolsheviks almost to a man, offers indisputable testimony of the vitality of revolutionary traditions among the masses as well as of their growing discontent.

Petty bourgeois democrats of the West, having but yesterday assayed the Moscow Trials as unalloyed gold, today repeat insistently that there is "neither Trotskyism nor Trotskyists within the USSR." They fail to explain, however, why all the purges are conducted under the banner of a struggle with precisely this danger. If we are to examine "Trotskyism" as a finished program, and, even more to the point, as an organisation, then unquestionably "Trotskyism" is extremely weak in the USSR. However, its indestructible force stems from the fact that it expresses not only revolutionary tradition, but also today's actual opposition of the Russian working class. The social hatred stored up by the workers against the bureaucracy—this is precisely what from the viewpoint of the Kremlin clique constitutes "Trotskyism." It fears with a deathly and thoroughly well-grounded fear the bond between the deep but inarticulate indignation of the workers and the organisation of the Fourth International.

The extermination of the generation of Old Bolsheviks and of the revolutionary representatives of the middle and young generations has acted to disrupt the political equilibrium still more in favour of the right, bourgeois wing of the bureaucracy and of its allies throughout the land. From them, i.e., from the right, we can expect ever more determined attempts in the next period to revise the socialist character of the USSR and bring it closer in pattern to "Western civilisation" in its fascist form.

From this perspective, impelling concreteness is imparted to the question of the "defence of the USSR." If tomorrow the bourgeois-fascist grouping, the "faction of Butenko," so to speak, should attempt the conquest of power, the "faction of Reiss" inevitably would align itself on the opposite side of the barricades. Although it would find itself temporarily the ally of Stalin, it would nevertheless defend not the Bonapartist clique but the social base of the USSR, i.e., the property wrenched away from the capitalists and transformed into state property. Should the "faction of Butenko" prove to be in alliance with Hitler, then the "faction of Reiss" would defend the USSR from military intervention, inside the country as well as on the world arena. Any other course would be a betrayal.

Although it is thus impermissible to deny in advance the possibility, in strictly defined instances, of a "united front" with the Thermidorian section of the bureaucracy against open attack by capitalist counterrevolution, the chief political task in the USSR still remains the *overthrow of this same Therrnidorian bureaucracy*. Each day added to its domination helps rot the foundations of the socialist elements of economy and increases the chances for capitalist restoration. It is in precisely this direction that the Comintern moves as the agent and accomplice of the Stalinist clique in strangling the Spanish Revolution and demoralising the international proletariat.

As in fascist countries, the chief strength of the bureaucracy lies not in itself but in the disillusionment of the masses, in their lack of a new perspective. As in fascist countries, from which Stalin's *political* apparatus does not differ, save in more unbridled savagery, only preparatory propagandistic work is possible today in the USSR. As in fascist countries, the impetus to the Soviet workers' revolutionary upsurge will probably be given by events outside the country. The struggle against the Comintern on the world arena is the most important part today of the struggle against the Stalinist dictatorship. There are many signs that the Comintern's downfall, because it does not have a *direct* base in the GPU, will precede the downfall of the Bonapartist clique and the Thermidorian bureaucracy as a whole.

A fresh upsurge of the revolution in the USSR will undoubtedly begin under the banner of the struggle against *social inequality and political oppression*. Down with the privileges of the bureaucracy! Down with Stakhanovism! Down with the Soviet aristocracy and its ranks and orders! Greater equality of wages for all forms of labour!

The struggle for the freedom of the trade unions and the factory committees, for the right of assembly and freedom of the press, will unfold in the struggle for the regeneration and development of *Soviet democracy*.

The bureaucracy replaced the soviets as class organs with the fiction of universal electoral rights—in the style of Hitler-Goebbels. It is necessary to return to the soviets not only their free democratic form but also their class content. As once the bourgeoisie and kulaks were not permitted to enter the soviets, so now *it is necessary to drive the bureaucracy and the new aristocracy out of the soviets*. In the soviets there is room only for representatives of the workers, rank-and-file collective farmers peasants and Red Army men.

Democratisation of the soviets is impossible without legalisation of *soviet parties*. The workers and peasants themselves by their own free vote will indicate what parties they recognise as soviet parties.

A revision of *planned economy* from top to bottom in the interests of producers and consumers! Factory committees should be returned the right to control production. A democratically organised consumers' co-operative should control the quality and price of products.

Reorganisation of the *collective farms* in accordance with the will and in the interests of the workers there engaged!

The reactionary *international policy* of the bureaucracy should be replaced by the policy of proletarian internationalism. The complete diplomatic correspondence of the Kremlin to be published. *Down with secret diplomacy!*

All political trials, staged by the Thermidorian bureaucracy, to be reviewed in the light of complete publicity and controversial openness and integrity. Only the victorious revolutionary uprising of the oppressed masses can revive the Soviet regime and guarantee its further development toward socialism. There is but one party capable of leading the Soviet masses to insurrection—the party of the Fourth International!

Down with the bureaucratic gang of Cain-Stalin!
Long live Soviet democracy!
Long live the international socialist revolution!

Ironically one of the groups denounced as "Trots" by the government rejected this analysis. They regarded the USSR as already capitalist so did not know what to do about the massive privatisation

> which took place

Against Opportunism and Unprincipled Revisionism

The politics of Leon Blum's party in France demonstrate anew that reformists are incapable of learning anything from even the most tragic lessons of history. French Social Democracy slavishly copies the politics of German Social Democracy and goes to meet the same end. Within a few decades the Second International intertwined itself with the bourgeois democratic regime, became, in fact, a part of it, and is rotting away together with it.

The Third International has taken to the road of reformism at a time when the crisis of capitalism definitely placed the proletarian revolution on the order of the day. The Comintern's policy in Spain and China today — the policy of cringing before the "democratic" and "national" bourgeoisie—demonstrates that the Comintern is likewise incapable of learning anything further or of changing. The bureaucracy which became a reactionary force in the USSR cannot play a revolutionary role on the world arena.

Anarcho-syndicalism in general has passed through the same kind of evolution. In France the syndicalist bureaucracy of Leon Jouhaux has long since become a bourgeois agency in the working class. In Spain, anarcho-syndicalism shook off its ostensible revolutionism and became the fifth wheel in the chariot of bourgeois democracy.

Intermediate centrist organisations centred about the London Bureau represent merely "left" appendages of Social Democracy or of the Comintern. They have displayed a complete inability to make head or tail of the political situation and draw revolutionary conclusions from it. Their highest point was the Spanish POUM, which under revolutionary conditions proved completely incapable of following a revolutionary line.

The tragic defeats suffered by the world proletariat over a long period of years doomed the official organisations to yet greater conservatism and simultaneously sent disillusioned petty bourgeois "revolutionists" in pursuit of "new ways." As always during epochs of reaction and decay, quacks and charlatans appear on all sides, desirous of revising the whole course of revolutionary thought. Instead of learning from the past, they "reject" it. Some discover the inconsistency of Marxism, others announce the downfall of Bolshevism. There are those who put responsibility upon revolutionary doctrine for the mistakes and crimes of those who betrayed it; others who curse the medicine because it does not guarantee an instantaneous and miraculous cure. The more daring promise to discover a panacea and, in anticipation, recommend the halting of the class struggle. A good many prophets of "new morals" are preparing to regenerate the labour movement with the help of ethical homeopathy. The majority of these apostles have succeeded in becoming themselves moral invalids before arriving on the field of battle. Thus, under the aspect of "new ways," old recipes, long since buried in the archives of pre-Marxian socialism, are offered to the proletariat.

The Fourth International declares uncompromising war on the bureaucracies of the Second, Third, Amsterdam and Anarcho-syndicalist Internationals, as on their centrist satellites; on reformism without reforms; democracy in alliance with the GPU; pacifism without peace; anarchism in the service of the bourgeoisie; on "revolutionists" who live in deathly fear of revolution. All of these organisations are not pledges for the future, but decayed survivals of the past. The epoch of wars and revolutions will raze them to the ground.

The Fourth International does not search after and does not invent panaceas. It takes its stand completely on Marxism as the only revolutionary doctrine that enables one to understand reality, unearth the cause behind the defeats and consciously prepare for victory. The Fourth International continues the tradition of Bolshevism which first showed the proletariat how to conquer power. The Fourth International sweeps away the quacks, charlatans and unsolicited teachers of morals. In a society based upon exploitation, the highest moral is that of the social revolution. All methods are good which raise the class consciousness of the workers, their trust in their own forces, their readiness for self-sacrifice in the struggle. The impermissible methods are those which implant fear and submissiveness in the oppressed before their oppressors, which crush the spirit of protest and indignation or substitute for the will of the masses—the will of the leaders; for conviction—compulsion; for an analysis of reality—demagogy and frame-up. That is why Social Democracy, prostituting Marxism, and Stalinism—the antithesis of Bolshevism—are both mortal enemies of the proletarian revolution and its morals.

To face reality squarely; not to seek the line of least resistance; to call things by their right names; to speak the truth to the masses, no matter how bitter it may be; not to fear obstacles; to be true in little things as in big ones; to base one's program on the logic of the class struggle; to be bold when the hour for action arrives—these are the rules of the Fourth International. It has shown that it could swim against the stream. The approaching historical wave will raise it on its crest.

Against Sectarianism

Under the influence of the betrayal by the historical organisations of the proletariat, certain sectarian moods and groupings of various kinds arise or are regenerated at the periphery of the Fourth International. At their base lies a refusal to struggle for partial and transitional demands, i.e., for the elementary interests and needs of the working masses, as they are today. Preparing for the revolution means to the sectarians, convincing themselves of the superiority of socialism. They propose turning their backs on the "old" trade unions, i.e., to tens of millions of organised workers—as if the masses could somehow live outside of the conditions of the actual class struggle!

They remain indifferent to the inner struggle within reformist organisations — as if one could win the masses without intervening in their daily strife! They refuse to draw a distinction between the bourgeois democracy and fascism — as if the masses could help but feel the difference on every hand!

Sectarians are capable of differentiating between but two colours: red and black. So as not to tempt themselves, they simplify reality. They refuse to draw a distinction between the fighting camps in Spain for the reason that both camps have a bourgeois character. For the same reason they consider it necessary to preserve "neutrality" in the war between Japan and China. They deny the principled difference between the USSR and the imperialist countries, and because of the reactionary policies of the Soviet bureaucracy they reject defence of the new forms of property, created by the October Revolution, against the onslaughts of imperialism. Incapable of finding access to the masses. they therefore zealously accuse the masses of inability to raise themselves to revolutionary ideas.

These sterile politicians generally have no need of a bridge in the form of transitional demands because they do not intend to cross over to the other shore. They simply dawdle in one place, satisfying themselves with a repetition of the selfsame meagre abstractions. Political events are for them an occasion for comment but not for action. Since sectarians as in genera every kind of blunderer and miracle-man, are toppled by reality at each step, they live in a state of perpetual exasperation, complaining about the "regime" and the "methods" and ceaselessly wallowing in small intrigues. In their own circles they customarily carry on a regime of despotism. The political prostration of sectarianism serves to complement, shadow-like, the prostration of opportunism, revealing no revolutionary vistas. In practical politics, sectarians unite with opportunists, particularly with centrists, every time in the struggle against Marxism.

Most of the sectarian groups and cliques, nourished on accidental crumbs from the table of the Fourth International lead an "independent" organisational existence, with great pretensions but without the least chance for success. Bolshevik-Leninists, without waste of time, calmly leave these groups to their own fate. However, sectarian tendencies are to be found also in our own ranks and display a ruinous influence on the work of the individual sections. It is impossible to make any further compromise with them even for a single day. A correct policy regarding trade unions is a basic condition for adherence to the Fourth International. He who does not seek and does not find the road to the masses is not a fighter but a dead weight to the party. A program is formulated not for the editorial board or for the leaders of discussion clubs, but for the revolutionary action of millions. The cleansing of the ranks of the Fourth International of sectarianism and incurable sectarians is a primary condition for revolutionary success.

Open the Road to the Woman Worker! Open the Road to the Youth!

The defeat of the Spanish Revolution engineered by its "leaders," the shameful bankruptcy of the People's Front in France, and the exposure of the Moscow juridical swindles—these three facts in their aggregate deal an irreparable blow to the Comintern and, incidentally, grave wounds to its allies: the Social Democrats and Anarcho-syndicalists. This does not mean, of course, that the members of these organisations will immediately turn to the Fourth International. The older generation, having suffered terrible defeats, will leave the movement in significant numbers. In addition, the Fourth International is certainly not striving to become an asylum for revolutionary invalids, disillusioned bureaucrats and careerists. On the contrary, against a possible influx into our party of petty bourgeois elements, now reigning in the apparatus of the old organisations, strict preventive measures are necessary: a prolonged probationary period for those candidates who are not workers, especially former party bureaucrats: prevention from holding any responsible post for the first three years, etc. There is not and there will not be any place for careerism, the ulcer of the old internationals, in the Fourth International. Only those who wish to live for the movement, and not at the expense of the movement, will find access to us. The revolutionary workers should feel themselves to be the masters. The doors of our organisation are wide open to them.

Of course, even among the workers who had at one time risen to the first ranks, there are not a few tired and disillusioned ones. They will remain, at least for the next period as bystanders. When a program or an organisation wears out the generation which carried it on its shoulders wears out with it. The movement is revitalised by the youth who are free of responsibility for the past. The Fourth International pays particular attention to the young generation of the proletariat. All of its policies strive to inspire the youth with belief in its own strength and in the future. Only the fresh enthusiasm and aggressive spirit of the youth can guarantee the preliminary successes in the struggle; only these successes can return the best elements of the older generation to the road of revolution. Thus it was thus it will be.

Opportunist organisations by their very nature concentrate their chief attention on the top layers of the working class and therefore ignore both the youth and the women workers. The decay of capitalism, however, deals its heaviest blows to the woman as a wage earner and as a housewife. The sections of the Fourth International should seek bases of support among the most exploited layers of the working class; consequently, among the women workers. Here they will find inexhaustible stores of devotion, selflessness and readiness to sacrifice.

Down with the bureaucracy and careerism! Open the road to the youth! Turn to the woman worker! These slogans are emblazoned on the banner of the Fourth International. *Under the banner of the Fourth International!*

Under the Banner of the Fourth International!

Sceptics ask: But has the moment for the creation of the Fourth International yet arrived? It is impossible, they say, to create an International "artificially"; it can arise only out of great events, etc., etc. All of these objections merely show that sceptics are no good for the building of a new International. They are good for scarcely anything at all.

The Fourth International has already arisen out of great events: the greatest defeats of the proletariat in history. The cause for these defeats is to be found in the degeneration and perfidy of the old leadership. The class struggle does not tolerate an interruption. The Third International, following the Second, is dead for purposes of revolution. Long live the Fourth International!

But has the time yet arrived to proclaim its creation? ... the sceptics are not quieted down. The Fourth International, we answer, has no need of being "proclaimed." It exists and it fights. It is weak? Yes, its ranks are not numerous because it is still young. They are as yet chiefly cadres. But these cadres are pledges for the future. Outside these cadres there does not exist a single revolutionary current on this planet really meriting the name. If our international be still weak in numbers, it is strong in doctrine, program, tradition, in the incomparable tempering of its cadres. Who does not perceive this today, let him in the meantime stand aside. Tomorrow it will become more evident.

The Fourth International, already today, is deservedly hated by the Stalinists, Social Democrats, bourgeois liberals and fascists. There is not and there cannot be a place for it in any of the People's Fronts. It uncompromisingly gives battle to all political groupings tied to the apron-strings of the bourgeoisie. Its task—the abolition of capitalism's domination. Its aim - socialism. Its method—the proletarian revolution.

Without inner democracy—no revolutionary education. Without discipline — no revolutionary action. The inner structure of the Fourth International is based on the principles of *democratic centralism*: full freedom in discussion, complete unity in action.

The present crisis in human culture is the crisis in the proletarian leadership. The advanced workers, united in the Fourth International, show their class the way out of the crisis. They offer a program based on international experience in the struggle of the proletariat and of all the oppressed of the world for liberation. They offer a spotless banner.

Workers—men and women—of all countries, place yourselves under the banner of the Fourth International. It is the banner of your approaching victory!

> **In the 1930s workers had suffered repeated defeats and socialists were reduced to a minority. Until recently socialists were a minority in the UK. However the dreamers were those who thought capitalism was practical! - DM**

Printed in Great Britain
by Amazon